# EAMON DE VALERA

## A DIAGNOSIS.

*Dr. M. Collins.* "A SOMEWHAT OBSCURE COMPLAINT. SAY '99.' "

*Mr. De Valera.* "I AM SORRY, SIR, BUT I CAN NEVER PROCEED ANY FURTHER THAN '98."

Historical Association of Ireland
Life and Times Series, No. 3

# Eamon de Valera

## PAURIC TRAVERS

*Published for the*
HISTORICAL ASSOCIATION OF IRELAND
*By* Dundalgan Press Ltd.

*First published* 1994
ISBN 0-85221-123-6

*For*
*Eamon and Elizabeth*

*Cover design:* Jarlath Hayes
Historical Association of Ireland, Dublin
*Printed by* Dundalgan Press, Dundalk

# FOREWORD

This series of short biographical studies published by the Historical Association of Ireland is designed to place the lives of leading historical figures against the background of new research on the problems and conditions of their times. These studies should be particularly helpful to students preparing for Leaving Certificate, G.C.E. Advanced Level and undergraduate history examinations, while at the same time appealing to the general public.

CIARAN BRADY
EUGENE J. DOYLE
*Historical Association of Ireland*

# PREFACE

I am grateful to Mary Moore, to my colleagues in the History Department at St Patrick's College, Drumcondra, James Kelly and Patrick O'Donoghue, and to Eoghan Ó Súilleabháin for their suggestions, advice and comments on an earlier version of this text. I also gratefully acknowledge the assistance of the librarians and archivists under whose auspices I have worked, especially Dr Breandán Mac Giolla Choille for facilitating access to the de Valera papers. I should also acknowledge the authors of the many specialist works without which a short study such as this would not be possible.

PAURIC TRAVERS
*History Department*
*St Patrick's College, Drumcondra*

# CONTENTS

# CHRONOLOGY OF DE VALERA'S LIFE AND TIMES

1882    14 Oct.: Born in New York.
1885    Brought back to Ireland; raised by his mother's family at Bruree, County Limerick.
1891    Death of Parnell.
1898    Scholarship to Blackrock College.
1904    Graduates from Royal University with a pass degree in Mathematics.
1908    Joins Gaelic League.
1910    Marries Sinéad Flanagan.
1912    11 April: Third Home Rule Bill introduced.
1913    Joins Irish Volunteers, established 25 Nov.; becomes commandant, 1915.
1915    Joins I.R.B.
1916    Easter Rising. De Valera commands 3rd Battalion of Volunteers. Sentence of death commuted to life imprisonment.
1917    June: released from prison. 11 July: elected M.P. for East Clare. 25 Oct.: elected President of Sinn Féin. 27 Oct.: elected President of Volunteers.
1918    April: member of Mansion House Conference. 17 May: arrested in 'German plot' arrests. Dec.: general election, elected for East Clare and East Mayo (where he defeated John Dillon), but defeated in Belfast by Joe Devlin.
1919    3 Feb.: escapes from Lincoln jail. 1 April: elected President of Dáil. Visits America, June 1919–Dec. 1920.
1921    July: negotiations with Lloyd George in London. July–Oct.: protracted correspondence regarding the terms of reference for any formal negotiations. Oct.–Dec.: Treaty negotiations.
1922    7 Jan.: Treaty approved by Dáil. 28 June: Civil War begins with attack on Four Courts.
1926    May: Fianna Fáil established.
1927    June: Fianna Fáil wins 44 seats. 11 Aug.: Fianna Fáil deputies take seats in Dáil. Sept.: Fianna Fáil wins 57 seats.
1932    Fianna Fáil assumes power with 72 seats; de Valera Taoiseach 1932–48, 1951–4, 1957–9. Sept.–Dec.: President of League of Nations. 'Economic war' begins.
1933    Oath of allegiance and right of appeal to Privy Council abolished.

1

| | |
|---|---|
| **1934** | Supports admission of Soviet Union to League of Nations. |
| **1935** | Supports sanctions against Italy. |
| **1936** | External Relations Act removes role of crown from Irish affairs. Supports non-intervention in Spanish Civil War. |
| **1937** | New constitution. |
| **1938** | Anglo-Irish Trade Agreement; return of Treaty ports. |
| **1939–45** | Irish neutrality during Second World War. |
| **1948** | Inter-party government replaces Fianna Fáil. |
| **1949** | Ireland becomes a republic. |
| **1951** | Fianna Fáil returns to power. |
| **1954** | Second inter-party government. |
| **1957** | Fianna Fáil returns to power. |
| **1959** | Resigns as Taoiseach and leader of Fianna Fáil. Elected President; re-elected 1966. |
| **1973** | Retires. Ireland joins EEC. |
| **1975** | 29 Aug.: dies. Buried at Glasnevin, Dublin. |

# INTRODUCTION

One day late in 1966, when no doubt the dust had settled on the fiftieth anniversary celebrations of the 1916 rising, Eamon de Valera rang the Folklore Department in U.C.D. to congratulate Seán Ó Súilleabháin on a lecture which had been broadcast the previous evening. Speaking in 'quite fluent but faintly ungrammatical Irish', de Valera proceeded to tell Ó Súilleabháin the story of the man who had no story. He recalled an incident from his primary school days when he and a friend, Martin Callaghan, took some time off school (probably mitching) to watch some itinerant tailors at work. One of the tailors asked Callaghan to tell a story, but he did not know any. So the tailor told the story of John Connors of Bruree.

At a 'rambling house' one night Connors had been asked to tell a story, but didn't have any. He went out to fetch water and encountered three men carrying a coffin. They asked him to help carry the coffin more evenly. When he asked who was in the coffin, they whispered that it was the Devil. They came to a house, but didn't enter when they heard the rosary being said within; at the next house they were welcomed in God's name, so the Devil roared at them to proceed; finally they came to a house where the husband and wife could be heard fighting, and the Devil said that was the house for him. When they put the coffin down on the doorstep, the three other bearers disappeared, so Connors hightailed it home. When he explained to his friends what had happened, they told him that never again could he say that he had no story.

Years later, in 1920, when de Valera was fund-raising in the United States, Séamus MacManus, the Donegal writer, told him the same story which he had heard from a travelling man in Donegal the previous year. The traveller was Martin Callaghan, de Valera's school-mate. MacManus commented that this was surely the makings of another story, 'The Two Boys from Bruree', one of whom became President of Ireland, while the other became a travelling man.[1]

Eamon de Valera could never be accused of having no story. So much has been written about him over the years that one may question whether there is anything more to be said or at least whether anything fruitful can be said in a short general study such as this. However, much of what has been written even recently, about de Valera is in the nature of attack or defence history. The Treaty split and Civil War made it difficult to be dispassionate. Books by Macardle, Gwynn, O'Faolain, Ryan, McManus and others, while teeming with insight, all fitted this category.[2] The genre culminated with the official biography by Longford and O'Neill in 1970 and the more useful Irish version by O'Neill and Ó Fiannachta.

Then fashions changed and heroes went out of fashion. More recently, however, there has been a return to biography, albeit of a more critical type, with major biographies of Parnell, Wolfe Tone and O'Connell among others. Tim Pat Coogan's recent work promised to add de Valera's name to the list, but its tone is closer to the old school, although as it presents the case for the prosecution rather than for the defence. De Valera still awaits a full-scale, dispassionate biography, although it is all the more necessary now that his memory has faded and he seems increasingly less relevant in the new restless Ireland of the final years of the twentieth century. This study does not purport to fill that gap. What it does seek to do, in keeping with the aims of the series, is to reassess de Valera's career in the context of recent research and from the perspective of a new era.

# 1

## BACKGROUND AND PERSONALITY

Ireland's national story as written for most of this century has been dominated by outstanding personalities, heroes, leaders, demigods who have only been pipped in the popularity stakes in the pages of popular history books by the various rebellions. Whether this dominance of particular individuals was due to the mediocrity of their contemporaries or to something in the mentality of the long colonised that demands a hero, an uncrowned king as it were, is a matter of debate. Whatever the reason, one cannot ignore the outstanding figures, and one such is Eamon de Valera.

By virtue of his longevity alone—his active political career spans almost sixty years—de Valera ranks among the major figures of the twentieth century. Few other international politicians of comparable standing spent as long in the political limelight. Judged by the criterion of longevity, even Winston Churchill, with whom he crossed swords on more than one occasion, appears as something of a pygmy.

There are few major events in twentieth-century Irish political history in which de Valera was not involved. He was one of the nationalist revival generation, but unlike the other 1916 leaders and many of those prominent in the War of Independence, he lived on through the Civil War to play an active part in the history of the new state. It is partly for this reason that he has always been such a controversial figure—one who produced feelings of either intense loyalty or distrust, one who was either revered or reviled. Even the most apolitical of people could not remain disinterested. Had he been executed in 1916 or killed in the War of Independence or Civil War, his place in the pantheon of Irish heroes would have been guaranteed; his name would certainly evoke less mixed emotions. However, the central fact of his political life was his survival.

Although he was a self-proclaimed idealist, he repeatedly proved himself to be in his own way a pragmatic politician. It fell to him more than any other politician to transform the idealism of the independence movement into the reality of a viable independent state. One suspects that when the emotions generated by the Civil War have been long since forgotten, de Valera will be judged not by what he did or did not do in 1916 or 1921, but rather on whether as the most powerful man in Ireland in the half-century after independence, he realised the aims of the independence movement.

* * * * * *

The boy from Bruree with whom this study is concerned could more accurately be called the boy from Lexington Avenue. Eamon de Valera was born in the Nursery and Child's Hospital, Lexington Avenue, New York, on 14 October 1882. His mother was Catherine Coll, an Irish immigrant from Bruree, County Limerick, and his father Vivion Juan de Valera, a Spaniard whose family was involved in the sugar trade between Spain, America and Cuba. Kate Coll registered her son's name as George but christened him Edward—he did not call himself Eamon until his entry into public life many years later.

Kate Coll had emigrated in 1879 and worked as a domestic servant. Throughout Eamon de Valera's life, stories persistently surfaced that Kate Coll had been pregnant when she emigrated and that her first son was conceived in Ireland. No reliable evidence has surfaced to support these stories. Such documentation as exists and the available chronology suggest that the stories have no basis in fact. It is less easy to refute the suggestion that Kate Coll and Vivion de Valera were never married and that Eamon de Valera was illegitimate. No record of the claimed marriage has ever been found. However, it may be unwise to read too much into the absence of documentation, and there seems no particular reason to doubt the official account. According to that version, de Valera's parents were parted when in 1884 his father was forced to move to the healthier air of Denver for health reasons. He died in the following year. Kate Coll returned to work and sent her young son back to Ireland to be reared by her mother.[1]

The Coll family home was a single-room thatched cottage, but they moved to a somewhat bigger but still humble labourer's cottage built as part of a Liberal government scheme in 1885. This rural, west of Ireland background helped to shape de Valera's outlook and beliefs. Romantic nationalists generally embraced a vision of an Ireland which was simple, rustic and spiritual and a counterpoise to urban, industrial and debased society elsewhere.[2] In de Valera's case this outlook may have been entrenched by his own experience of having been removed by force of circumstances from urban America to rural Ireland and by the continued need, in response to the jibes of his opponents, to demonstrate that he was fully Irish. Desmond Ryan, one of his earliest biographers, argues that a key to de Valera's whole character is provided by childhood impressions of

> the stormy eighties, a faint recollection of the United States, Spanish American forebears with a touch of Viking blood, the hills of East Limerick, with crumbling coastline, patriotic legends, memories of Sarsfield and the Gaelic heroes, in an area within twenty miles of the Shannon, an old seat of the Gaels and Normans, warriors and monks, as nourishment for dreams and excursions.[3]

While Ryan's picture is undoubtedly overly romantic, his view is confirmed by de Valera's own testimony. At the height of the Treaty debates (at a time when his origins had been snidely commented upon) de Valera in a remarkable speech milked his Limerick background for the purposes of self-authentication:

> I have been brought up amongst the Irish people. I was reared in a labourer's cottage here in Ireland. I have not lived solely amongst the intellectuals. The first fifteen years of my life that formed my character were lived amongst the Irish people down in Limerick; therefore I know what I am talking about; and whenever I wanted to know what the Irish people wanted, I had only to examine my own heart and it told me straight off what the Irish people wanted.[4]

De Valera, or Eddie Coll as he was now known, attended the local National School and then went to the Christian Brothers' School in Charleville, seven miles' walk from Bruree. At sixteen, when he was considering returning to America, he won a scholarship to Blackrock College in Dublin. He also contemplated joining the priesthood at this time, but was advised to wait until he finished his schooling. By then the notion had passed.

One aspect of de Valera's political style which has fairly been traced to his schooldays is his penchant for splitting hairs. His real passion at school was mathematics. It was his best subject at school and he took it for his degree at the Royal University, later teaching mathematics at Rockwell and Belvedere College before becoming a lecturer in Carysfort in 1906. In his political and military career he never lost the didactic style and what one biographer described as a 'predeliction for the manipulation of abstract concepts' and another identified as a tendency to reduce everything to a formula, often a very abstract formula indeed.[5] He certainly had a keen awareness of semantics and repeatedly sought to use the ambiguity and imprecision of language to his advantage.

De Valera's fondness for formulae was sometimes an asset, as, for example, in October 1917 when he helped to produce the formula which resolved the divisions within the different wings of Sinn Féin, allowing republicans and non-republicans to unite behind a constitution which pledged Sinn Féin to the achieve-ment of a republic and to then put it to the people to decide whether they wanted it or not. (It may be argued, of course, that this was simply to store up trouble for the future—as indeed proved to be the case.) In 1918 de Valera again devised a useful formula pledging those who opposed conscription to resist it by the most effective means at their disposal; this was vague enough to be acceptable to constitutionalists, bishops and Volunteers. Perhaps his success in these cases emboldened de Valera to believe that a formula could be found to solve all conflicts; if so, he was to fail disastrously in 1922: Document No. 2 and the concept of 'external association' came too late and were never sufficiently understood by anyone other than de Valera himself, who was unable to get the point across to those who mattered.

A great irony of de Valera's long career is that he was, or at least professed to be, a reluctant politician. Such professions of detachment and disinterest are, of course, not unusual—Parnell, de Gaulle and even Hitler routinely adopted similar poses—but in de Valera's case it was at least consistent. In a school debate at

Blackrock he supported the motion that a constitutional monarchy was preferable to a republic with the argument that constant elections disturb the people.[6] Although he supported Redmond and Home Rule until 1912, he shared the nationalist revival generation's suspicion of parliamentarianism and party politics. In 1914, when the Volunteers split on the question of the war, he sided against Redmond because he felt the Volunteers should be independent. In 1917 he was initially against the tactic of contesting elections and was reluctant to stand himself in Clare. During the Treaty debates he declared himself sick and tired of politics and promised to withdraw from party politics no matter what happened.[7]

In the event, the rejection of his line in the Treaty debates and the defeat in the Civil War propelled de Valera even more firmly into the realm of party politics. He passed on to Fianna Fáil the rhetoric of the old Sinn Féin movement which insisted that it did not speak for any sectional interest but for the nation as a whole. Hence the paradox that the more Fianna Fáil became in practice the classic example of the modern professional political party, the more de Valera insisted that it was not a political party at all but a national movement.

As well as this fine distiction between a political party and a national movement, de Valera drew a distinction between national sovereignty and majority rule. In his school debate at Blackrock he concluded that no rule could be more tyrannical than majority rule. A quarter of a century later, in 1926, he described the Treaty split as having been between majority rule and national sovereignty and insisted that he had no choice but to defend national sovereignty.[8] How the national will was to be determined if majority rule was to be disregarded was never clearly specified, if one discounts looking into his own heart or appealing to the dead generations.

Physically, de Valera was a big, even awkward man with plain features, whose appearance has sometimes been compared to that of Abraham Lincoln—a comparison which would have pleased him, as Lincoln's photograph hung in his study. Like Parnell, he was not a natural orator, but despite—or perhaps because of—an austere, detached manner, he had a strong presence and could make a powerful impact.[9] His first contact with the old-guard leadership of the nationalist movement was at the Mansion House anti-conscription conference in April 1918. William O'Brien recalled his impression:

> His transparent sincerity, his gentleness and equability captured the hearts of all. His gaunt frame and sad eyes deeply buried in their sockets had much of the Dante-esque suggestion of 'the man who had been in hell'. His was that subtle blend of virility and emotion which the Americans mean when they speak of a 'magnetic man'.[10]

When he first heard him speak in New York in 1920, W. B. Yeats was also impressed but rather less enthusiastic. He described de Valera as

> a living argument rather than a living man. All propaganda, no human life, but not bitter, hysterical or unjust. I judged him persistent, being both patient and energetic, but that he will fail through not having enough human life as to judge the human life in others.[11]

## 2

## SOLDIER, POLITICIAN, SOLDIER, 1912–23

As with so many of his generation, de Valera's initiation into the nationalist movement was through the Gaelic League. He joined the Ard-Chraobh of the Gaelic League in 1908, beginning an enthusiasm for the Irish language which endured throughout his life. One of his teachers was Sinéad Flanagan, whom he married in 1910. He became convinced during the Home Rule crisis that concessions could not be won without a show of force. He attended the inaugural meeting of the Irish Volunteers on 25 November 1913, joined the new organisation and quickly became captain of the Donnybrook company. He took to this task enthusiastically and prepared a training manual for his company. When the split occurred in the Volunteer movement, he supported the minority breakaway group on the grounds that the Volunteers could be most effective if they were independent of politics.

When plans got under way for a rebellion before the war ended, de Valera was made commandant of the 3rd Battalion of the Irish Volunteers and adjutant of the Dublin Brigade. He declined to join the executive of the Volunteers on the grounds that it might take him away from his command. For a long time he also refrained from joining the I.R.B. for the same reason and because he disapproved of secret oath-bound societies. This created an anomalous situation, as some of his own junior officers were members and the I.R.B. controlled the Volunteer executive. He was eventually persuaded by Thomas MacDonagh to allow himself to be sworn in, but he refused to attend meetings.[1]

Despite his reluctance to join the I.R.B., de Valera had already concluded that a rebellion was inevitable and had promised his support. Unlike Pearse and some of the other leaders, he did not consider that it should be a blood-sacrifice, a token gesture to awaken nationalist sentiment. He believed that if they were able to hold out in Dublin for any length of time, it might serve to spark a rebellion throughout the country. The thoroughness of his preparations for the rising bears this out. His battalion was assigned to the south-eastern approaches to the city. In the weeks before the rising he walked every street and lane in the area. This advance preparation stood his battalion in good stead during Easter week.[2]

Because of Eoin Mac Néill's countermanding order, only about 130 of his normal strength of 500 men turned out, many of them badly armed. The absentees included some senior officers. Despite this, the battalion was easily the most successful in the rising, inflicting more than half the British casualties. Although hugely outnumbered, de Valera's battalion with its headquarters at Boland's Mills successfully prevented reinforcements from the Sherwood Foresters regiment from reaching the city for a number of days. The battalion was also the last to surrender, only giving up the fight after Pearse's surrender order had been confirmed by Thomas MacDonagh.[3] If de Valera was a reluctant politician, he was an enthusiastic soldier. It is clear that he relished his involvement with the Volunteers, at least before 1916. His somewhat stern, dogmatic personality suited him for leadership, and in his approach to the rising he displayed both an appetitite for and a proficiency in military matters. There is some (disputed) evidence that by the end of Easter week de Valera was overwrought and in a state of nervous exhaustion, which, considering the circumstances, would hardly be surprising. Yet such indications of human frailty, even if well established, hardly dimish the record of his Boland's Mills garrison.[4]

De Valera was not a signatory of the proclamation read by Pearse at the G.P.O.; indeed, he did not even see a copy of that document until long after the rising. However, as a commandant of a battalion, and especially the battalion responsible for so many casualties, he fully expected to be executed. His court martial was delayed for a number of days while the more senior leaders were tried and executed. In the meantime the public reaction against the executions had begun to grow, and the government informed General Maxwell that only the ringleaders should be executed. The executions of Connolly and MacDonagh proceeded, but de Valera and Thomas Ashe had their sentences commuted to life imprisonment. It has sometimes been suggested that de Valera was spared, following an approach by his wife to the American consul, because of his American birth, but the surviving records reveal nothing to contradict his own view that he was spared simply because the government had decided that the executions had served their purpose.[5]

Between 1916 and 1921 de Valera emerged as the undisputed leader of the radical nationalist movement. As the most senior surviving leader of the rising, he was seen by many as being the living embodiment of that movement. In immediate practical terms, that meant that he assumed the leadership of his fellow-prisoners in Dartmoor, Lewes and Maidstone prisons. He insisted that they maintain Volunteer organisation and discipline. On his release in June 1917, he considered himself first and foremost a Volunteer and declared the Volunteers the inheritors of the mantle of 1916. For all that, he did not have a fully coherent view of how to proceed. While still in prison he strongly opposed the suggestion from outside that Joseph McGuinness, a fellow-prisoner, should be put forward as a candidate for a by-election in Longford. His stance was based partly on the fear of the demoralisation which would be caused by defeat and partly on his distrust of orthodox politics.

Even after McGuinness's victory de Valera remained unconvinced about the tactic. On his release from prison, he was invited to contest the East Clare by-election, but only agreed to stand under pressure from colleagues. In an election speech he rationalised his change of mind:

> Political platforms have little attraction for me, but in this case I considered that the principles for which my comrades died were at stake, and that it was my duty, seeing I still adhered to these principles, to avail of every opportunity to vindicate and advance them.[6]

Although de Valera insisted that if there was 'a fair chance of military success', he would take arms again, the East Clare by-election was a significant change of direction in his career. His easy victory gave a boost to the policy of contesting elections which culminated in Sinn Féin's triumph at the general election in December 1918, when de Valera was returned for East Clare and East Mayo and was only narrowly defeated by Joe Devlin in Belfast. It also marked a transition in de Valera's career from soldier to politician.

Looked at in retrospect, the ascendancy of Sinn Féin (and the I.R.A.) in the post-1916 period seems inevitable. At the time the changeover was more confused and uncertain. That a radical nationalist movement would emerge was likely; what was less certain was the shape it would take and how it would proceed. Well into 1917 different organisations were claiming to represent advanced nationalist opinion. One of de Valera's achievements, ironic though it may be in the light of later developments, was to unify the various wings and avoid the possibility of a debilitating split. Within Sinn Féin the simmering tensions between doctrinaire republicans, dual monarchists and pragmatists were defused by his proposal that the constitution be amended to contain the following provision:

> Sinn Féin aims at securing the international recognition of Ireland as an independent Irish republic. Having achieved that status, the Irish people may by referendum freely choose their own form of government.[7]

Arthur Griffith generously agreed to step down, and de Valera became President of Sinn Féin on 25 October 1917. Two days later he was elected President of the Volunteers. De Valera thus united the political and military movements under his leadership. Only the I.R.B., with which he had severed his connections, remained outside his nominal control. The policy which had slowly emerged was, as Constance Markievicz put it, a combination of the policy of Tone and Parnell: a constitutional movement backed by physical force. De Valera shared this view: he told one election meeting: 'We fight England for freedom with votes, and then, if we fail, with rifles if necessary.'[8]

Six months after becoming President of Sinn Féin and the Volunteers, de Valera's skills were severely tested when the government announced its intention to extend conscription to Ireland. When the Irish Parliamentary Party failed to defeat the measure in the House of Commons, a conference of nationalists was arranged for the Mansion House to organise a united front against conscription. De Valera and Arthur Griffith represented Sinn Féin at the conference. De Valera was not overawed by the more seasoned representatives of the Irish Party. In the matter of the anti-conscription pledge, he outflanked all potential opposition by showing it in advance to the Archbishop of Dublin and

gaining his approval. He then used Archbishop Walsh's imprimatur to persuade the reluctant representatives of the Irish Party
to accept the pledge, which met the needs both of the constitutionalists, who were wary of being associated with violent methods,
and of the Volunteers, who were likely to resist conscription by
force no matter what was decided. Later that day he reversed his
strategy, using the support of the politicians to persuade the
assembled bishops at Maynooth to accept the pledge. When they
raised the possibility that the Volunteers might resist by force, de
Valera replied strongly that the Volunteers would resist by force, if
necessary, no matter what the bishops said.[9]

The idea of a united nationalist front of bishops, parliamen-
tarians and Volunteers to resist conscription was initially viewed
with suspicion by members of Sinn Féin and was opposed by
Michael Collins and the I.R.B., but de Valera was strongly in
favour. In the event, it proved a personal triumph for himself and
for Sinn Féin. He even managed to persuade the Mansion House
conference that all financial aid to those who suffered in the resistance to conscription should be administered by the National Aid
Association, the republican welfare organisation which had
administered relief to the families of those involved in the rising.
Although conscription was not implemented, the threat resulted
in a rush of membership for both Sinn Féin and the Irish
Volunteers.[10] It gave Sinn Féin a new political respectability which
bore fruit in the triumph at the 1918 general election. However, it
also provided the crucial impetus to covert preparations for
guerrilla war, a war with which de Valera was to have very little
direct involvement. The ending of the First World War, the
general election and the meeting of the first Dáil all diverted
attention from the extent to which the roots of the War of
Independence lie in the anti-conscription movement.

De Valera's emergence as the political leader of the nationalist
movement after 1916 coincided with a growing distancing of
himself from many of the most active soldiers. He sought to create
a broad national movement which would have a political and, if
necessary, a military focus, but his main role was in the former
rather than the latter. It is significant that when the Sinn Féin
leaders were forewarned in May 1918 about the government's
intentions to arrest them on foot of a so-called 'German plot', it

was decided that they should not seek to evade arrest. The political capital to be made outweighed the loss of leadership. The 'German plot' arrests served both to emphasise de Valera's political importance and to drive the Collins-led military wing of the movement under ground.

By the time of de Valera's spectacular escape from Lincoln prison in February 1919 the situation in Ireland had been transformed. Sinn Féin had won its desired mandate in the general election, Dáil Éireann had assembled, and the first shots had been fired in the War of Independence. On his return to Ireland, de Valera was elected President of the Dáil and was almost immediately dispatched to America to raise funds and to promote the international recognition of the Republic.

The vigour of de Valera's later protestations that he was not a politician is probably partly explained by the extent to which he had come to be identified as *the* leader of the political wing of the movement in this period. His enforced isolation from events in Ireland—he was in jail from May 1918 to February 1919 and in America from June of that year to December 1920—meant that even in the political sphere his role was more symbolic than real. It is in that context that his mission to America, judged by many historians as at best a qualified success, must be viewed. He met with enthusiastic receptions and was given the freedom of the city of New York, but could persuade neither the Republican nor Democratic parties to support recognition of the Republic. His efforts were not helped by the fact that he had alienated influential Irish-American leaders and spent a good deal of time embroiled in in-fighting with Irish-American groups. Eventually he established his own organisation, the American Association for the Recognition of the Irish Republic, which raised a considerable amount of money for the cause.[11]

It is clear that de Valera was uneasy about his prolonged absence in the United States, but he was persuaded that he should remain. Not surprisingly, when he did return to Ireland, he was out of touch with events, as is illustrated by his repeated pressing for a change in military tactics in the war, from guerrilla tactics to large-scale conventional military engagements. The subsequent attack on the Custom House was a military disaster, involving the loss of one hundred I.R.A. members through casualties and arrests in a single day.[12] Later he attempted to reorganise the army 'on a regular basis', with closer control exercised by the cabinet and the Minister for Defence. This met with considerable resistance from the most active soldiers, and an open conflict was averted only because of the signing of the Treaty.[13]

### Settlements and Divisions

De Valera's return from America facilitated the advent of peace negotiations. With British attention turning at last to the inevitability of talks, de Valera was identified as the main political leader with whom it might be possible to do business. The fact that when Lloyd George finally came to 'shake hands with the murder gang', it was de Valera he sought is testimony to the latter's success in maintaining the position he had inherited as a result of 1916. The only doubt on the British side was whether he could in fact control the militants.[14] Although de Valera was officially on the run, the British decided that, in order to facilitate peace moves, he should not be arrested. When he was arrested by accident on 22 June 1921, he was immediately released.

In response to Lloyd George's invitation to talks, de Valera consulted with his cabinet colleagues and unsuccessfully sought a meeting with James Craig. A truce was hastily arranged which came into operation on 11 July. Three days later de Valera was in London. In the course of the following week four meetings took place between de Valera and Lloyd George, but they did not get much beyond preliminary skirmishing. Lloyd George played the role of the elder statesman and tried to overawe the younger man. Showing a straight bat throughout, de Valera effectively blocked the Prime Minister's manoeuvring, and his handling of these negotiations was solid and assured. His official biographers concluded accurately that if he gained nothing, he gave nothing away either. Lloyd George, who described negotiating with him as being like riding a merry-go-round always one horse behind, would probably have agreed. His main tactic was to get Lloyd George to make an offer which might be brought back to the Dáil. Lloyd George duly obliged, offering Ireland dominion status, but with specified limitations, particularly in the area of trade. Although the document expressed support for Irish unity, the proposal would only apply to Northern Ireland with the consent of the northern parliament. De Valera dismissed this proposal and left without the document, only to send a messenger back for it later.[15]

There ensued a protracted correspondence between de Valera and Lloyd George which continued until late September aimed at establishing the basis for a full-scale conference. The letters of both leaders were repetitive and meandered through the realms of history and political theory. Perhaps for the first time, however, they did force de Valera to formulate his ideas more precisely. His main objection to dominion status was that, for reasons of its proximity to Britain, Ireland could never in practice enjoy the status of a dominion. He told Lloyd George in London that he would be willing to accept the status enjoyed by New Zealand or Canada in practice, a status which he considered was a product of their distance from Britain. As a means of giving effect to this, he began to develop the notion of 'external association', under which Ireland might be an independent country within the British Commonwealth. However, external association was never fully worked out, and it lacked the simple clarity and appeal of 'the Republic'.

The key stumbling-block in the way of a conference was de Valera's insistence that the Irish delegates would be representatives of a sovereign government and Lloyd George's equally emphatic rejection of this. Finally it was agreed that there would be no preconditions. As de Valera put it, it was 'precisely because neither side accepts the position of the other that there is a dispute at all, and that a conference is necessary to search for and discuss such adjustments as might compose it'.[16] Lloyd George's invitation to a conference in London to discuss 'how the association of Ireland with the community of nations known as the British Empire may be reconciled with Irish national aspirations' was formally accepted by de Valera on 30 September, and the conference opened on 11 October 1921.[17]

When the Dáil cabinet discussed the composition of the delegation to go to London, de Valera proposed that Griffith should lead with Collins as his deputy. They in turn suggested that he should go. The cabinet split evenly on the matter, which was settled by de Valera's own casting vote. An attempt was then made in the Dáil to reverse this decision. The issue of whether de Valera should have gone to London has been a source of considerable debate. The majority of historians, like the majority of his colleagues, have tended towards the view that his absence from the delegation was a mistake: as Oliver MacDonagh puts it, de Valera was in America when he should have been in Ireland, and in Ireland when he should have been in London. Desmond Williams concluded that it was the greatest mistake of his life.[18] As things turned out, that may well have been so; but his own rationale of keeping himself in reserve to allow a fall-back position and to be better placed to prevent a split with the hardline republicans in the event of a compromise settlement did make some sense, particularly if one accepts the view that de Valera was willing to compromise and only rejected the Treaty because he did not like that particular compromise.[19]

If one assumes that de Valera was willing to compromise, a more pertinent criticism of him may be the failure to impress his views on the delegation in any detail. If the intention of holding himself in reserve was to allow the delegation to play for time, then this was not sufficiently clear to or accepted by the delegation. Even allowing for the heat of battle, the absence of a more carefully worked out Irish strategy seems remarkable; as the acknowledged political leader, de Valera must bear some of the responsibility for this. As late as 3 December, when the delegation discussed the draft Treaty with the cabinet in Dublin, the discussion lacked direction and the outcome was confused.[20]

De Valera'a response to the Treaty was influenced by the sense of personal betrayal he felt, not least about the manner in which he heard that it had been signed—he was in Limerick and heard the news by telephone. He was surprised that agreement had been reached so soon and assumed that the British side must have made concessions. It was only on his return to Dublin on the evening of 6 December that he received full details. However, there is no reason to suppose that he was not genuinely convinced that a better deal was possible, if not on Ulster, then at least in the central areas effecting sovereignty. Kathleen O'Connell, his secretary, recorded in her diary on 7 Decemeber 1921:

> Treaty published in all the papers this morning. P. [President] in an awful state. Oh! What a disappointment to our bright hopes—what a fiasco. Cabinet meeting at 11.30.

President was thinking of recalling delegation and asking for resignation of Cabinet ministers—Griffith, Collins, and Barton. G's [Griffith's] statement about Freedom such a farce. Partition of our country and British subjects is the 'freedom' we have got.[21]

The cabinet accepted the Treaty by four votes to three, so de Valera carried the fight to the Dáil. The Treaty was discussed over thirteen days of public and private debate before and after Christmas. It was finaly approved on 7 January 1922 by 64 votes to 57. De Valera dominated the debate, speaking or intervening more than 250 times.[22] His mood and tone ranged from anger to sadness and disappointment, from displays of high-handedness and pedantry to a resigned acceptance of defeat. At the end of the debate, after the Treaty had been approved and when Collins called for unity, de Valera rose to speak but quickly broke down sobbing.[23]

De Valera conceded that what separated the two sides was very small, but he did not think that Britain would go to war for 'that small difference'.[24] That small difference related to dominion status and the oath of allegiance, and de Valera tried to resolve it by presenting (and later amending) his Document No. 2. The major differences between this and the Treaty were that it asserted that Ireland would be a sovereign country associated with the Commonwealth on matters of common concern, removed the oath, and limited the British control over the Treaty ports. It left the partition issue virtually unchanged (see below, pp 35–8).

The Treaty split has often been characterised as a division between principle and pragmatism, but that is over-simplistic. De Valera was not a diehard who opposed all compromise. Much of his manoeuvring in the months before the Treaty was signed was based on the assumption that some compromise was possible. In his correspondence with Lloyd George he had barely mentioned the Republic. Earlier, before allowing his name to go forward for re-election as President, he expressly warned that he did not consider that the republican oath bound him to that form of government. He accepted office only on the understanding that no road was barred and that every method could be considered. Those who could not agree with that could resign.[25] As the Treaty split deepened and de Valera's public utterances became less moderate and he became identified more and more as a hardliner, the subtleties of his earlier position were forgotten. Two days after the Dáil's approval of the Treaty de Valera and the cabinet resigned. His reappointment was immediately proposed, but he was defeated by 60 votes to 58. Arthur Griffith was elected in his place. De Valera and his supporters withdrew in disgust, denying the right of the majority to betray national sovereignty. That remained de Valera's essential position for the rest of his career.

The acceptance of the Treaty by the cabinet and the Dáil left de Valera the politician in a dilemma which he took a long time to resolve. There was no reason to believe that the population at large would reverse the verdict. The only option, apart from acquiescence, was armed resistance. De Valera was extremely uncomfortable with this, and, in any case, his influence with the armed men on either side was small. He made some attempts during 1922 to retrieve the situation, but his leadership was indecisive and haphazard. In a number of speeches for which he has been widely criticised he warned of the consequences which would follow the Treaty. He told an audience at Thurles in March 1922 that the Volunteers would have to complete their fight for independence

> not over the bodies of foreign soldiers, but over the dead bodies of their own countrymen. They would have to wade through Irish blood, through the blood of the soldiers of the Irish government and through, perhaps, the blood of some of the members of the government in order to get Irish freedom.[26]

Even if viewed as a prediction rather than a threat, the language was, at the very least, unwise. However, de Valera can hardly be blamed for the series of events which culminated in the Civil War. He was not involved in the decision of anti-Treaty soldiers to occupy the Four Courts on 14 April 1922. Far from confrontation, he agreed an election pact with Collins on 20 May to prevent the forthcoming elections to the new Dáil sparking off open conflict. It may well have been that de Valera feared another rebuff. It could also be argued that Dáil elections were exactly the place for resolving the central issue and that political conflict was preferable to war. De Valera certainly did not seek the latter, and the most serious accusation that could be levelled against him was that he abdicated his political responsibilities and, by failing to chart a political course, allowed the initiative to pass to the military.

With the attack on the Four Courts by the troops of the Provisional Government, the Civil War began.[27] Having failed in his attempts to undo the Treaty by other means, de Valera threw in his lot with the anti-Treaty forces, not as their leader but as an ordinary soldier. He symbolically washed his hands of affairs by resigning as President of the Volunteers and re-enlisting as a private. If this was intended to foreshadow his promised withdrawal from politics, then the resolve did not last long.

3

## RECUPERATION, 1923–32

Between 1921 and 1923 de Valera went from being the acknowledged political leader of nationalist Ireland to being an isolated, divisive figure, trusted neither by Free Staters nor by extreme republicans and the gunmen.[1] In the light of the extent of the severity of the rebuff he received, his recuperation and ascent thereafter is remarkable. When he emerged from hiding after the Civil War, he was arrested and spent a year in prison. He used that time well to reflect on his position and how best to restore his fortunes.

In the aftermath of the defeat of the anti-Treaty forces in the Civil War it was decided to reorganise the old Sinn Féin party as the political voice of republicans with de Valera as President. The new party faced an immediate test in the shape of the general election of August 1923. De Valera emerged from hiding to contest the election, but was quickly arrested. Despite this and the continued imprisonment of many of its members, Sinn Féin attracted considerable support, particularly in the west of Ireland, and managed to win 44 seats.[2] This initial surge in support was also reflected at local level, but it was not sustained. Its policy of not taking its place in the Dáil made it difficult for Sinn Féin to be more than a 'helpless spectator'.[3] The party declined and fared badly in a series of by-elections in 1925.

De Valera became convinced that a change of direction was needed. The débâcle over the Boundary Commission which resulted in the entrenching of partition strenghtened his argument in favour of the necessity for a republican presence in the Dáil. In January 1926 he announced that if the oath of allegiance was removed, he would enter the Dáil. Two months later he put a motion before the Sinn Féin Ard-Fheis confirming that if the oath was removed, entry into the Dáil would become a matter of policy, not principle. When the Ard-Fheis narrowly rejected his motion, de Valera resigned as President of Sinn Féin and quickly established a new party, Fianna Fáil.[4] This not only allowed a change of heart on abstention but gave de Valera unfettered control, which he had not enjoyed within Sinn Féin.

De Valera's process of recuperation is, of course, closely associated with the establishment of Fianna Fáil in 1926. That gave him what he lacked in 1921, a strong power base. The general outline of the story of the rapid growth of Fianna Fáil, and its transformation into a well-oiled political machine which has dominated Irish politics ever since, is well known, although, strangely, we still lack a good, comprehensive party history. Such a study might *inter alia* try to distinguish how much of the party's success was de Valera's and how much was a product of astute party management by others. One suspects that it was a combination of both. Either way, the Fianna Fáil party is certainly one of de Valera's more enduring achievements.

The Fianna Fáil party was established at the La Scala Theatre in Dublin and grew rapidly. It benefited from the stature of de Valera and from the fact that it brought with it from Sinn Féin public representatives and a party structure on which it could build. De Valera immediately embarked on a nationwide tour to galvanise support. Under the direction of Gerald Boland and Seán Lemass, the party quickly built up an unrivalled local, constituency and national organisation which has provided much of the basis for its electoral success ever since. The three-tier structure of local *cumainn* in each parish, a constituency organisation and a national executive derived from the structure of Sinn Féin and, earlier, of Parnell's party.

| 1927 Jun. | 1927 Sept. | 1932 | 1933 | 1937 | 1938 | 1943 | 1944 | 1948 |
|---|---|---|---|---|---|---|---|---|
| 44 (*153*) | 57 | 72 | 77 | 69 (*138*) | 77 | 67 | 76 | 68 (*147*) |

| 1951 | 1954 | 1957 | 1961 | 1965 | 1969 | 1973 | 1977 | 1981 |
|---|---|---|---|---|---|---|---|---|
| 69 | 65 | 78 | 70 (*144*) | 72 | 75 | 69 | 84 (*148*) | 78 (*166*) |

| 1982 Feb. | 1982 Nov. | 1987 | 1989 | 1992 |
|---|---|---|---|---|
| 81 | 75 | 81 | 77 | 68 |

Seats won by Fianna Fáil in Dáil elections. (The figure in brackets is the total number of seats in the Dáil; it is given only at those points where it was changed.)

Of course, political machines of themselves do not guarantee electoral success. Fianna Féil adopted a range of political and social policies aimed at consolidating the support of republicans and appealing in socially radical terms to the labouring and lower middle class, especially in rural areas and in the towns. The six main points in its programme were: the reunification of the country as a republic; the restoration of the Irish language and culture; the harnessing of the resources of the country for the benefit of all the people; the achievement of economic independence to make Ireland self-sufficient; the establishment of as many families as practicable on the land; and an intensive programme of rural industrialisation to counteract the drift to the cities.[5]

This Fianna Fáil programme was first placed before the electorate in the general election of June 1927, when it won 44 seats, three fewer than Cumann na nGaedheal, which had lost sixteen seats. Sinn Féin, de Valera's old party, won only five seats. When his supporters were refused admission to the Dáil because they refused to take the oath, de Valera sought to initiate a referendum to have the oath abolished. Following the assassination of the Vice-President of the Executive Council and Minister for Justice and for External Affairs, Kevin O'Higgins, the government forced his hand. It introduced two bills requiring all election candidates to commit themselves in advance to take their seats if elected and removing the possibility of a referendum to abolish the oath. De Valera identified the choice facing his party now as entry into the Dáil or abandonment of politics. They chose the former. On 11 August 1927 de Valera and his followers entered the Dáil. They signed the book containing the oath presented by the Clerk of the Dáil while simultaneously affirming that they were taking no oath and that what was involved was an empty formality.[6] On such fine distinctions rests the foundation of modern Irish political democracy.

De Valera's embrace of democratic politics was at first conditional and qualified. As Seán Lemass explained in a Dáil speech in 1928, Fianna Fáil was a 'slightly constitutional party'. They had taken the course they had because it seemed to promise success; if they did not succeed in achieving their aims, then they might revert to other methods.[7] In the event, however, the new approach was to prove spectacularly successful and transformed the political situation. When the government narrowly survived a motion of no confidence, a new election was called. In the general election of September 1927 Fianna Fáil won 35 per cent of the votes and 57 seats, to 37 per cent and 61 seats for Cumann na nGaedheal. Only the support of a number of smaller parties enabled the government to stay in power.

During the next five years Fianna Fáil continued to develop its organisation and to enhance its appeal. De Valera's commitment to end the payment of land annuities to the British exchequer struck a responsive chord both with nationalists and with small farmers. The basis of de Valera's objection to the annuities was that the British government had in 1925 renounced all financial claims on the Free State rather than a fundamental objection to annuities *per se*, but the distinction mattered little to the small farmers, who hoped to benefit from a renunciation of repayments. Fianna Fáil's espousal of popular economic and social policies, and in particular the promise of protectionism and self-sufficiency, met with increasing enthusiasm as the economic depression of the late 1920s deepened and the Cosgrave government ran out of steam.

The establishment of the *Irish Press* in 1931 represented another important step in the rise of Fianna Fáil. The existing national newspapers were hostile to Fianna Fáil. The *Irish Press*, controlled by the de Valera family and actively supporting the de Valera line, helped to redress the balance. It quickly achieved a circulation of 100,000 and played an important role in the election of February 1932, when the prospect of a Fianna Fáil victory generated a virulent propaganda campaign linking the party with gunmen and communists. In the event, Fianna Fail won 45 per cent of the vote and 72 seats, to 35 per cent and 56 seats for Cumann na nGaedheal. Significantly, support for Fianna Fáil, which had previously been strongest in the west and south-west of Ireland, had grown elsewhere too, with more then fifty per cent support in Longford, Westmeath and Monaghan. Fianna Fail was well on the way to becoming a national rather than simply a west of Ireland party.[8] When de Valera formed his first government on 9 March 1932, he completed a remarkable transformation in his fortunes. The question that remained was how he would use the power he had achieved.

# 4

## POWER, 1932–48

The accession to power of Fianna Fáil in 1932 marked a triumph for de Valera and an important watershed in Irish political democracy. That a peaceful transition took place at all is significant and, whatever the teething problems, a credit to both sides. This triumph was followed by a succession of others during the 1930s as de Valera engaged in his relentless pursuit of sovereignty. The abolition of the oath of allegiance in 1933, the removal of the right of appeal to the Privy Council in the same year, the diminution and ultimately, in 1937, the abolition of the Governor-Generalship, the removal of the king from the constitution in 1936, and in 1937 the replacement of the Free State constitution itself were all landmarks on the road to making Ireland a republic in all but name. The fact that the more de Valera succeeded the more he proved the validity of Collins's 'stepping-stone' interpretation of the Treaty only partially diminishes the achievement.

In all these cases de Valera revealed a preoccupation with the form and symbols as much as the realities of independence. However, he also displayed a clever tactical awareness and a shrewd sense of when to act and how far to go. To the consternation of the British government, he acted mostly within the letter of the law. Ironically, the abolition of the oath was made possible by the Statute of Westminster of 1931, for which the Free State government could take much credit. De Valera used constitutional precedent to force the king to dismiss the Governor-General and replace him with his own nominee, Domhnall Ó Buachalla, a shopkeeper from Maynooth. The Governor-General, theoretically the symbol of the crown, now became the symbol of the new order in Ireland. The abdication crisis in 1936 gave de Valera another opportunity, this time to remove all mention of the king in the constitution. All these steps were part of de Valera's avowed policy of dismantling the Treaty and culminated in the new constitution adopted by referendum in July 1937 which came into effect from 29 December 1937.

27

## Economic Policy

It may be argued that in his self-righteous pursuit of his constitutional agenda de Valera neglected the economic essentials of independence, but that is hardly surprising. That de Valera saw economics as secondary to politics is illustrated by the 'economic war', which may be deemed as politically satisfying and economically disastrous. In that context, the undoubted achievement of the Anglo-Irish Trade Agreement of 1938 loses some of its gloss.

The so-called 'economic war' of 1932–8 was ostensibly a product of the conflict generated by de Valera's policy of withholding the land annuities repayable to the British exchequer under the land purchase acts. In reality the annuities issue presented the occasion for a conflict which both sides relished. The British government was keen to avail of the first opportunity to emasculate de Valera, whom it continued to view as a dangerous extremist; de Valera, for his part, saw the opportunity to implement the Fianna Fáil economic programme in ideal conditions.[1]

De Valera's withholding of the annuities was met with the imposition of a 20 per cent tariff on most Irish exports by the British government which generated a similar imposition on British goods by de Valera. The main casualties were large cattle farmers, who were unlikely to have supported Fianna Fáil in any case, but the whole agricultural community was affected.[2] Although the impact was serious, the economic war proved popular, and de Valera won a decisive victory at the general election of January 1933. Armed with this mandate and with the added impetus of the tariff war, he proceeded to implement the Fianna Fáil economic programme. The war dragged on until 1938, when the British agreed to accept a once-off payment of £10 million in settlement of the annuities issue. In two associated compacts it was agreed to ease restrictions on trade between the two countries and that the Treaty ports should be handed back to the Irish state. The latter agreement opened the way for the unfettered exercise of neutrality.

Fianna Fáil's economic policy was essentially a development of the Sinn Féin programme of economic nationalism. In practice this meant the development of agriculture, particularly through the encouragement of tillage, and the fostering of native industry.

There was an impressive growth in wheat production in the 1930s, but at the expense of other tillage crops. The livestock industry suffered badly from the effects of the economic war, although the consumer benefited from falling meat prices.[3]

De Valera added to existing tariff barriers a further series of protective measures such as the Control of Manufactures Act of 1932. The Industrial Credit Company was established in 1933 to aid industrial development. Séan Lemass, the Minister for Industry and Commerce, enthusiastically adopted the Cosgrave government's model of using semi-state companies controlled indirectly by the government wherever these could be usefully employed to promote industrialisation and general ecomomic development. The Irish Sugar Company, Bord Fáilte, Aer Lingus and Bord na Móna were all established during this period. In the social sphere, the Housing Act of 1932 provided assistance for house-building, and 132,000 houses were built in the next decade. Unemployment assistance was introduced in 1933, and widows' and orphans' pensions in 1935, both at very modest rates.[4]

By the 1950s de Valera's programme of self-sufficiency and protectionism provided Ireland with no more than the frugal sufficiency he desired, but it is doubtful, given the state of the international economy, whether any other policy would have fared better. One recent economic historian has concluded that industrial policy in the 1930s was better geared towards generating employment throughout the country in the short run than towards building up a self-supporting Irish industrial sector.[5] The modest growth of home industry behind protective barriers was counterbalanced by the decline in agricultural employment. However, the intervention of the Second World War makes it difficult to calculate exactly how the equation would have balanced out.

### Foreign Affairs and Neutrality

In these years de Valera achieved considerable success in the area of foreign affairs, not least in establishing that foreign affairs meant more than simply Anglo-Irish relations. He maintained a strong interest in international relations and personally retained the External Affairs portfolio in his government. He actively tried to use the League of Nations to establish Ireland's independent position. He was a genuine and consistent advocate of the rights of small nations and of the value of an organisation like the League in regulating international relations and guaranteeing collective security. It was only when the League had conspicuously failed to defend weaker nations in a series of cases in the 1930s that he came round to the view that Ireland's best, indeed only, foreign policy option was neutrality.

De Valera's first speech to the League of Nations was as President of the Assembly in September 1932. In a remarkably frank address he startled his audience by listing the criticisms being made of the League and questioning its effectiveness. The League had failed to prevent or end the Japanese intervention in China in the previous year. De Valera called for a strengthening of the League with equality of states large and small instead of the political and economic interests of larger powers determining action.[6]

De Valera brought to the League and foreign policy generally a strong sense of the rights of small nations and a commitment to the regulation of international relations by principles of justice and fair play rather than by might. He was rapidly disillusioned. The Italian invasion of Abyssinia in 1935 presented a test case both for the League and for de Valera. Strong action against Italy would be unpopular in Ireland because Italy was a Catholic country and because it was sponsored by Britain. To his credit, de Valera resolved the dilemma by sticking to his principles and supported the case for strong action against Mussolini. He told the Assembly of the League that Abyssinia represented the final test: if the sovereignty of even the weakest country was taken away with impunity, then 'the whole foundation of the League would crumble into dust'.[7]

In May 1936 Abyssinia was formally annexed by Italy. In June de Valera told the Dáil that the failure of the League in Abyssinia had left small nations with no option but to look to their own defence. Referring to the build-up of tension in Europe, he expressed the general desire of the Irish people to remain neutral.[8] In July 1936 the League decided to withdraw sanctions against Italy. Speaking in the debate in Geneva, de Valera declared that the League had suffered a bitter humiliation:

. . . the small states are powerless. As I have already said, peace is dependent upon the will of the great states. All the small states can do, if the statesmen of the greater states fail in their duty, is resolutely to determine that they will not become the tools of any great power and that they will resist with whatever strength they possess every attempt to force them into a war against their will.[9]

De Valera's disillusionment with the League of Nations and growing commitment to neutrality can also be seen in the attitude he adopted to the Spanish Civil War when, despite pressure at home, he refused to recognise Franco's regime.[10]

There is no question but that de Valera saw neutrality in terms of principle rather than opportunism. His success in maintaining neutrality was only possible because the people of the Irish state were similarly persuaded. De Valera's famous rebuff of Churchill at the end of the war took its force precisely from the moral basis of his argument. In a victory speech in May 1945 Churchill bitterly condemned Irish neutrality and gratuitously added that if it had been necessary, Britain would have forcibly seized Irish ports. De Valera responded with firmness but restraint in a memorable radio broadcast:

It seems strange to me that Mr Churchill does not see that this, if it be accepted, would mean that Britain's necessity would become a moral code and that . . . other people's rights were not to count. It is quite true that other great powers believe in this same code in their own regard and have behaved in accordance with it. That is precisely why we have the disastrous succession of wars—World War No. 1 and World War No. 2—and shall it be World War No. 3? . . . It is indeed hard for the strong to be just to the weak. But acting justly always has its rewards.[11]

As we have seen, de Valera considered that the failure of the League of Nations left a small country which had recently won its independence with no option but to pursue a neutral stance in a conflict between the major powers. The fact that one of the major powers involved was Britain made neutrality even more likely given the history of animosity and suspicion in Anglo-Irish relations, but it seems certain that de Valera would have opted for neutrality even if Britain had not been involved. De Valera saw neutrality not as an end in itself but as an expression of independence, and his position was wholeheartedly supported by the vast majority of the people of the Irish state.[12] That position has also been supported by most historians, even those not naturally sympathetic to de Valera, who have seen neutrality as the ultimate exercise in independence. One exception is F. S. L. Lyons, who has interpreted de Valera's stance in the war not as an expression of independence but as an abandonment of Ireland's place in the society of nations and a regrettable turning towards isolation.[13]

Irish neutrality, then, was not a new policy in 1939. It had emerged in the 1920s (and indeed before) and was repeatedly articulated by de Valera in the 1930s once the League of Nations had failed. Another rationale for neutrality offered by de Valera was partition. He told the Dáil in May 1939 that neutrality was the only policy acceptable to the majority as long as partition lasted. Partition was certainly a consideration, not least given the possibility of conscription being introduced in the north. It strengthened de Valera's unwillingness to co-operate in alliance with Britain. Paradoxically, however, partition made neutrality more viable. The presence of British and U.S. bases in Northern Ireland diminished the strategic importance of the south of Ireland in the Allied war effort. This made action against the Irish state, which both the British and Americans considered at different times, less likely.

The experience of the First World War, when initial Irish sympathy quickly gave way to hostility and contributed to the success of Sinn Féin, also weighed with de Valera. He was mindful of the threat which the I.R.A. might pose if given a propaganda weapon. The experience of 1914–18 deeply ingrained the nationalist reluctance to become involved in 'Britain's war'.

Yet another factor often cited in the decision to remain neutral was the military one: lack of readiness. There is no question that in military terms the Irish state was woefully unprepared for involvement in an international conflict. At least in the early years of the war, the popular slogan that Ireland was ready to defend her shores was only true in the psychological sense. However, lack of preparedness did not prevent the involvement of other countries in the war and, like the I.R.A. threat, cannot be considered a significant reason for neutrality.

As with so much in Anglo-Irish relations, the rhetoric of neutrality was very different from the reality. The release of Irish, British and American government records of the period have confirmed that in practice Ireland was 'neutral on the Allied side'. De Valera assured Britain at the outbreak of the war that Ireland would not be used as a base for attack on Britain. In August 1939 he told Dr Hempel, the German minister in Dublin, that for reasons of geography and economic considerations Ireland would show 'a certain consideration' for Britain. That certain consideration involved the return of captured British airmen while captured Germans were interned, and continuous high-level military and intelligence co-operation.[14] Irish sympathy was strongly with the Allies in the war, but de Valera maintained the diplomatic niceties to the end, even to the perverse extent of visiting the German legation to express his sympathy on the death of Hitler.

Whether one sees it as the ultimate expression of independence, the ultimate expression of Irish anglophobia, or a retreat into Plato's cave, de Valera's embrace of neutrality was not casual or opportunist. The Irish position had been made clear well in advance and was widely supported by all Irish parties. For this and for his clear-sightedness and consistency in the face of British and American pressure de Valera can claim credit, although to describe it as his greatest achievement or his finest hour as some historians have done is to overstate the case.[15] As Joseph Lee argues, if one sees neutrality as an active rather than a passive position, one which did not necessarily mean isolation but which offered possible gains as well as losses in the political, diplomatic and economic spheres, the Irish exercise in neutrality failed to live up to its potential.[16]

# 5

## DE VALERA'S IRELAND?

Although Eamon de Valera was the most important man in Ireland in the half-century after independence, it is somewhat misleading to talk in terms of de Valera's Ireland or the de Valera dispensation as if he alone shaped or controlled society.[1] He did have a considerable influence in certain areas such as politics, government and the educational system. He certainly gave a tone to the Ireland of the 1930s, 1940s and 1950s with a vision of life, as Sean O'Faolain complained, 'so dismal as to make the regime of the trappist monks of Mount Melleray seem like a Babylonian orgy'.[2] However as de Valera was to find, many of the most fundamental realities of economy and society in Ireland were not so susceptible to change. These included a deep-rooted attachment to the maintenance of the family farm as an intact unit, even at the cost of emigration.

Notwithstanding Fianna Fail's commitment in 1926 to create a self-sufficient Ireland and in the process establish as many people as possible on the land, emigration was a permanent, almost essential, feature of Irish life in the forty years after independence. Political rhetoric or official government policy never acquired sufficient force to counterbalance the central features of the rural economy. The deeply entrenched commitment to landownership and maintenance of the family inheritance, and the concomitant of these, the avoidance of subdivision, proved more than a match for de Valera's visions of frugal sufficiency and communal values.

The depression of the 1930s and the popularity of protectionist policies kept emigration in check and helped de Valera to pursue his economic experiment. But when in the 1940s and 1950s the floodgates opened, the crisis which developed threatened not only to submerge de Valera's vision but to undermine a rural economy which had tolerated if not demanded emigration. In 1948 de Valera told a St Patrick's Day gathering of emigrants in

San Francisco that 'we shall soon be able to say that no man or woman need leave Irish soil because of economic necessity'. Two months earlier, on an election platform at home he was more circumspect: on the issue of emigration he conceded pessimistically that 'we cannot corral the people and say "you must not go out"'. In 1951, as the crisis deepened, he again admitted the limits of his power and gave an equally pessimistic diagnosis to Dáil Éireann. There were, he said, 'certain things you can do and certain things you cannot do. The truth is that, in the long run, the amount you can do is not very much.'[3]

One way of solving emigration which was widely discussed in government circles for many years was the promotion of earlier marriages. De Valera was convinced that the success of his party's policy of establishing as many families as possible on the land and thus ending emigration was dependent, *inter alia*, on persuading young women to marry into small farms. One approach which he favoured strongly was the notion of the state subsidising the building of dower houses, i.e. second houses which would be occupied by the inheriting son and his wife. He raised that possibility in the late 1920s and again in the 1930s. In 1943 he established an inter-departmental committee to implement what he clearly identified as his pet scheme. He again raised the matter in 1947 and 1951. Despite his continued sponsorship, the dower house scheme got nowhere.[4] Its failure illustrates well the limits of his power. Key elements in the rural economy outweighed de Valera's wishes or the desire to end emigration. The main objection to the dower house proposal was that two houses on a holding might lead to subdivision of the holding.[5]

### Partition

Although he often claimed that it was the prospect of partition which brought him into politics initially,[6] and in spite of the fact he genuinely regretted the division of the country, de Valera's Ireland was a partitioned Ireland. The reality of partition was more firmly entrenched at the end of his period of office than it was at the beginning. On Northern Ireland, as on so many issues, de Valera the dogmatist, the apparent doctrinaire, was in practice de Valera the pragmatist. As John Bowman has demonstrated, de Valera's political rhetoric on partition was one thing; his attitudes and actions in practice another. After a brief flirtation with the possibility of coercing Ulster in 1917–18, he concluded that force would not succeed. Not that he accepted partition: he shared the general nationalist view that the Irish nation would prove irrepressible and the new northern state unviable; in this view, unity was 'inevitable but postponable'.[7]

De Valera's view of the Ulster question when he first became active in politics was that it was mainly a product of British manipulation. In 1917–18 he conceded that Ulster Protestant grievances would have to be addressed, but insisted that they could not have a veto on independence. He insisted that he favoured conciliation but not concession. If northern Unionists refused to co-operate, then they were an 'alien garrison' and would have to be coerced.[8] During his eighteen months in America in 1919–20 de Valera presented a more accommodating view, still insisting on unity but holding out the posibility of concessions to meet Ulster Unionist fears. He maintained this approach on his return to Dublin in December 1920. In May 1921 he had discussions with James Craig the northern Unionist leader. No agreement was reached in the ninety minutes—Craig later recalled that most of the time was taken up with a history lecture by de Valera, after half an hour of which he had only got to Brian Boru—but the fact that the meeting took place at all is of some importance.[9]

During the preliminary discussions which took place after the truce de Valera made it plain that he would not accept the 'mutilation' of the country but that he was willing to concede local autonomy for Ulster within the context of an all-Ireland settlement and that he 'did not contemplate the use of force'.[10] Later in the Dáil de Valera again ruled out using force to coerce Ulster.[11] At the commencement of the Treaty negotiations in London his position was that he was willing to allow the six north-eastern counties to opt for a subordinate parliament within the Irish state. He complained that the Treaty signed on 6 December achieved neither unity nor independence. It is possible that he might have accepted the oath and dominion status if unity had been achieved, but as the Treaty split developed, his position hardened. His original Document No. 2 included all the same Ulster clauses as the Treaty but with a preamble asserting the unity of Ireland. He later removed these so as to allow discussion to focus on the other aspects of the Treaty.[12] As we have seen, this is what happened, with the Treaty debates focusing remarkably little on partition.

After the Treaty split, de Valera's stance on the north became somewhat less conciliatory and tended towards rhetoric. In the autumn of 1924 he staged a well-publicised visit to Belfast and was conveniently arrested and deported. Shortly afterwards he was arrested in Derry, refused to recognise the court, and was imprisoned for a month. During the Boundary Commission controversy he reiterated his willingness to accept an autonomous northern parliament within an all-Ireland state.[13] The failure of the Boundary Commission gave a powerful weapon which he used effectively against the government. It is not surprising that reunification of the country was stated so baldly as one of the fundamental aims of his new party. The establishment of Fianna Fáil and entry into the Dáil lost de Valera the support of some republicans, which may explain a hardening in his rhetoric regarding Ulster after 1926. He threatened to 'punish Ulster' economically and warned that peace would never come until partition was ended.

As usual, the reality was somewhat different from the rhetoric. Fianna Fáil declared itself an all-Ireland movement, but de Valera resisted strong pressure from his supporters to organise actively in the north. He told his party's first Ard-Fheis that

> they should take cognizance of the fact that conditions in the twenty-six counties and in the six counties were different and they required different treatment. The time to start organising in the six counties would depend on conditions there.[14]

That remained his position, notwithstanding his election as M.P. for South Down in 1933. De Valera was reluctant to intervene in northern affairs, and apart from regular mentions in political speeches, there is little evidence of the Ulster question being a top priority after he came to power. In 1937–8 there was an upsurge in activity, and again, for more understandable reasons, after the election defeat of 1948.

De Valera regarded partition as an economic, political and cultural disaster, but conceded that there was not much he could do about it. When he was asked in an interview in 1953 whether he expected to see an end of partition in his lifetime, he responded that while he used to think so, he could not now be so confident. It depended 'on events beyond any foretelling, and circumstances beyond my control'.[15] Ten years later he conceded in another interview: 'Ireland is Ireland without the North.'[16] Despite the claim in Article 2 of his 1937 constitution that 'the national territory consists of the whole island of Ireland', in practice de Valera's Ireland was the twenty-six-county unit, a fact conceded in Article 3 of the constitution, which limits the application of the constitution to twenty-six counties 'pending the reintegration of the national territory'. In the meantime, all that was possible was for the independent Irish state to create a society which would attract northern Unionists. In a pronouncement to the Dáil in 1933 de Valera provided a useful yardstick by which to judge the success of his own policy:

> The only policy for abolishing partition that I can see is for us, in this part of Ireland, to use such freedom as we can secure to get for the people of this part of Ireland such conditions as will make the people in the other part of Ireland wish to belong to this part.[17]

### Church and State

Any assessment of de Valera's career must of necessity come to terms with his attitude to religion. As is well known, he was a deeply committed Catholic. Todd Andrews described him as 'a deeply religious man but not evidently pious'.[18] He carried into his approach to politics a strong moral sense. The question of how he balanced his Catholicism and his political responsibilites requires more careful analysis than it has received.[19] Like the vast majority of politicians in Dáil Éireann, he viewed Ireland as fundamentally a Catholic country and saw no reason to insist on a rigid separation of church and state. Ireland, he declared in 1935, was a Catholic nation, and that was Ireland's destiny, and prevalent forms of state-worship would not flourish as long as people remembered that.[20] That view found its most eloquent expression in the 'special position' assigned to the Catholic Church in the 1937 constitution and the incorporation of Catholic social teaching in its social clauses.

However, the portrayal of de Valera as a religious fundamentalist is misleading. In fact he displayed a consistent pragmatism on the relationship of religion and politics. Like all nationalist politicians from O'Connell onwards, de Valera saw the need for the support of the clergy and was willing to court that support; but there were limits to his flexibility. Clerical indifference in 1916 and outright hostility during the Civil War and in the 1920s do not seem to have carried much weight with him. Nor is that surprising, given that de Valera in April 1918 had gone to Maynooth to tell the assembled Catholic bishops in forthright terms that the Irish Volunteers would resist conscription by force regardless of what the church might say. When in 1925 Seán Lemass declared that they were opening a campaign to destroy the political influence of the Catholic Church,[21] he does not seem to have received any reproach from his party chief.

De Valera was prone to exaggerate his clerical contacts, particularly with Archbishop Walsh. Before 1930 his influence with the hierarchy was limited. Thereafter, particularly during the 1930s, he sought and won clerical endorsement. However, while the influence of the Catholic Church was enhanced, there were definite limits. His espousal of the cause of Russian admission to the League of Nations in 1934, his support for sanctions against Mussolini's Italy in 1935 and his strong support for League neutrality in the Spanish Civil War in 1937, all against strong Catholic pressure, evidence the limits of clerical influence. Even the 1937 constitution itself, rightly cited as illustrating the power of the church, can up to a point be seen as evidence of the limits to its power, given that the papacy was unhappy that it did not go far enough.

Dr John Charles McQuaid, whom de Valera had consulted about certain aspects of the constitution, was critical of the constitution for 'admitting the false principle of the separation of church and state.'[22] McQuaid was overstating the case: de Valera's view, as T. P. O'Neill has argued, was that 'the rights and duties of the state and church were two circles, not separate but overlapping. In the area between the arcs which overlapped there needed to be consultation.'[23] In some cases consultation meant concession; in others it did not. In 1943 McQuaid clashed with de Valera over a church–state issue relating to the work of the Commission on Youth Employment, of which the archbishop was chairman. Despite a threat by McQuaid to resign, de Valera refused to back down. Not long afterwards de Valera took a hard line in the I.N.T.O. strike despite, or perhaps because of, intervention on the teachers' behalf by McQuaid. He saw the issue of teachers' salaries as one for the state, not for the church. Likewise he continued to grant state subvention to Trinity College despite clerical disapproval.[24]

De Valera was keen to resolve potential church–state conflicts before they became public. That was his attitude to the row which simmered behind the scenes from 1945 over the proposed Public Health Bill which boiled over in the shape of the Mother and Child controversy during the tenure of the inter-party government. Significantly with Fianna Fáil back in power, the matter was resolved behind the scenes in 1953. De Valera headed off a proposed condemnation of the new Fianna Fáil Health Act by Cardinal D'Alton, and a compromise was agreed under which the means test demanded by the bishops was included.[25]

## De Valera and Women

De Valera's attitude to and relationship with women is another matter requiring attention, not least as his constitution did so much to enshrine formally a Victorian perception of women's role in society. It hardly needs to be said that de Valera did not invent this perception. He did, however, elevate it to new heights.

While the aloof, formal de Valera attracted unwavering allegiance from many women, not least his devoted secretary of thirty-eight years, Kathleen O'Connell, he could hardly be accused of being a feminist. Gertrude Gaffney, one of the fiercest critics of that 1937 constitution, argued that he simply did not understand women. De Valera, she said,

> had always been a reactionary where women were concerned. He dislikes and distrusts us as a sex, and his aim ever since he came into office has been to put us in what he considers is our place, and to keep us there.[26]

It seems likely that de Valera's own background influenced his vigorous assertion of the domestic role of women. Abandoned by his mother, his own domestic life was for many years unusual. Sean O'Faolain in his 1933 portrait hints at the difficulty of maintaining normal domestic relations at a time of intense political and military activity:

One of the pictures that keeps reverting to my mind as I have been writing this Life is of Michael Collins playing on the carpet in de Valera's house with his little sons, while de Valera in some cold, formal, unhomely, gilded hall of the old Waldorf-Astoria in New York is thinking fondly of that house by the sea at Greystones, hearing over the chatter of fashionable American ladies of fashion and the nasal cacophony of a jazz-band the waves moaning with their double note of a rise and fall on the beach at Greystones, and seeing the light shining in his windows, and the homely, simple, warm domestic scene from which he was thousands of miles away.[27]

One of his sons later recalled that his own first recollection of a normal situation was 'to have my father in America and my mother at home', adding that his father at this time 'meant little more than the tall, dark-haired, bespectacled, severe figure who occasionally appeared on the home scene'.[28] Much of his time between 1916 and 1926 was spent in jail, in America, on the run or on the hustings.

De Valera's constitution sought to enshrine an ideal view of women and their role at a time when the reality for most women was very different. Gertrude Gaffney accused de Valera and his predominantly male government of being remote from the experience of women. De Valera had

never been in contact with, and will never descend to, the realities of life. He lives in a remote and distant political world of his own where his plans look exceedingly well on paper . . . If he had more contact with the average working man and woman he would know that ninety per cent of the women who work for their living in this country do so because they must.[29]

Following an energetic campaign by women's groups, de Valera agreed to amend his draft constitution slightly to meet some of the objections: that was as far as he was willing to go. However, the fact that the normally unyielding 'Chief' compromised at all is important and may be attributed to the pressure from two women for whom he had considerable respect, Dorothy Macardle and Louie Bennett.

De Valera's view of women's role in society was part of a wider vison of the ideal Ireland which was most famously outlined in his speech 'The Ireland That We Dreamed Of' broadcast on St Patrick's Day 1943:

That Ireland which we dreamed of would be the home of a people who valued material wealth only as a basis of right living, of a people who were satisfied with frugal comfort and devoted their leisure to the things of the spirit; a land whose countryside would be bright with cosy homesteads, whose fields and villages would be joyous with the sounds of industry, with the romping of sturdy children, the contests of athletic youths and the laughter of comely maidens; whose firesides would be forums for the wisdom of serene old age. It would, in short, be the home of a people living the life that God desires men should live.[30]

The central thrust of the speech, which commemorated the fiftieth anniversary of the establishment of the Gaelic League, was aimed at encouraging people to learn and use Irish. The rather austere social vision, while not out of character, was certainly influenced by the isolation of Ireland in a world tearing itself to pieces in armed conflict. This context is now forgotten, and the speech is usually cited to illustrate de Valera's lack of realism. His vision is now remote, if it was ever otherwise, but he might argue that at least a vision of the future, however romanticised, was publicly articulated.

# 6

## EXTINCT VOLCANO, 1948–75

Faced with the evidence of economic failure after the Second World War, both de Valera and Seán Lemass would claim that only the intervention of the war had thwarted the achievement of Fianna Fáil's economic aims. Oliver MacDonagh presents a more plausible interpretation:

> By 1939 Fianna Fáil seemed, temporarily at least, to have exhausted its creative purposes. The new democratic and constitutional systems had been established; republican symbolism had been imposed up to the level which de Valera considered prudent in the light of other national interests; the very modest measures of social reform which were consequential on the economic war and the party's dependence on workers' and small farmers' votes had been carried through with a decided air of finality; and the limitaions of protectionist industrialism of the old Sinn Féin variety had been thoroughly exposed. But the extinct volcanoes of 1939 were not to be disturbed for nine more years.[1]

In a perceptive 'Tourist Guide to Irish Politics' in 1947 the radical critic Peadar O'Donnell caught de Valera's and Fianna Fáil's dilemma precisely when he decribed the party as 'Treaty party no. 2, the party of the people, no longer in a position to make new gestures towards national sentiment and therefore unprotected against economic unrest: slipping'.[2] The 1948 general election, at which sixteen years of Fianna Fáil hegemony were brought to an end, was the first since independence at which economic issues played a dominant part. De Valera came to power in 1932 promising full employment and self-sufficiency. In 1948 he was called to account for his stewardship. Employment, emigration and the rising expectations of a new generation dominated the election, as they were to dominate the elections in 1951, 1954 and 1957.

Peadar O'Donnell's tourist guide identified the main threat to Fianna Fáil as coming from disillusioned de Valera supporters who were flocking in great numbers to the new socially radical

43

republican party Clann na Poblachta. The 1948 general election was called early in an attempt to head off this trend, but the tactic was only a partial success. Despite putting forward ninety candidates, Clann na Poblachta won only ten seats, fewer than they hoped and Fianna Fáil feared, but enough to give the combined opposition parties a chance to form a government. The setback ought to have prompted a fundamental reassessment within Fianna Fáil, but de Valera insisted on seeing the result as a quirk of the proportional representation system. He immediately embarked on a tour of the United States which he used to promote an anti-partition campaign. The twin themes of his speeches in America were the achievement of sovereignty in the south and the inequity of partition. There was little hint of the economic challenge facing the country.[3]

In the context of de Valera's career, perhaps the most significant development during the period of the first inter-party government was the declaration of the republic. For an issue which had so long dominated Irish politics, the formal declaration of a republic was something of an anticlimax. There was consternation within Fianna Fáil at being upstaged on the issue, and some deputies did threaten to oppose it on the grounds that it might make the ending of partition more difficult. However, de Valera insisted that what was involved in formally creating a republic was merely 'a demonstration to clear the air'. Ireland was in practice already a republic. He dismissed the possibility of it making unification more difficult, adding revealingly that

> Everything that we here, representing the majority of our nation, have done through the years in showing goodwill has been quite ineffective to get these people to advance to any sense of their responsibilities, either as regards justice or peace or good relations with their fellow-countrymen or good relations between Ireland and Britain.[4]

The disunity of the inter-party government meant that de Valera's period in the wilderness was brief, but the underlying change in Irish politics and society could not be reversed. When he returned to power in 1951, he insisted on retaining the conservative Seán MacEntee as Minister for Finance as if to emphasise that there would be no change. MacEntee's response to falling production, growing unemployment and a serious balance-of-payments deficit was cautious and orthodox in the extreme. The

1952 budget was more severe than any since de Valera first came to power, with sharp increases in both direct and indirect taxation. While these measures solved the immediate balance-of-payments problem, they did so at a political cost, and the underlying crisis remained.[5]

This government was probably the least effective of any led by de Valera to date, and it was no surprise when Fianna Fáil found itself back in opposition in 1954. This time, however, the sojourn was used to better effect. Seán Lemass later admitted that it was not until this second period of opposition that Fianna Fáil really got down to seriously thinking about the country's post-war economic problems and 'preparing our minds for a comprehensive approach to them'.[6] The party was divided on the best way forward, with some taking the cautious, orthodox line espoused by MacEntee, and others supporting the more innovative and expansionist policy of Lemass. This ideological split raged within the party throughout the 1950s, with MacEntee initially having the upper hand, and Lemass, for so long the heir apparent to de Valera, seeming to be out of favour. After the party's electoral defeat in 1954 the pendulum swung the other way. De Valera was remote from much of this economic debate, leaving it to his lieutenants, but he admitted in 1954 that the restoration of Fianna Fáil's electoral position depended on making inroads in urban areas, where MacEntee's budget had bitten hardest and where Lemass's appeal was greatest.

The 1950s decade was a period of instability and transition, with voters showing an impatience with the platitudes of earlier years. These changes left de Valera very much a survival of an earlier era. Although he was still Taoiseach when Fianna Fáil embarked on its change of economic direction on its return to government in 1957, he can have had little stomach for the abandonment of protectionism and self-sufficiency. He was by now seriously afflicted with eye problems, with the result that his role in the 1950s was reduced and indirect. In 1951 he had chosen not to retain the External Affairs portfolio. In 1952 he had a series of operations on his eyes which left him almost blind. Yet he soldiered on for seven more years, retiring as Taoiseach and party leader early in 1959.

One of his last political crusades was the attempt to replace the existing proportional representation system with a straight vote and single-member constituencies. In November 1958 he personally introduced the necessary legislation in the Dáil. Although rejected by the Seanad, the bill was passed, but by the time the matter came to referendum de Valera had resigned. The referendum and the poll for the presidency were held on the same day. The electorate displayed considerable sophistication: while the presidential election resulted in a victory for de Valera, the referendum was lost (as was a similar proposal in 1968). The major objection raised to the proposal to abolish proportional representation was that it was aimed to ensure the continued dominance of Fianna Fáil and might lead to single-party government. De Valera denied this and suggested that it would be as likely to benefit the major opposition party. He did admit, however, that it would militate against the proliferation of smaller parties and thus inter-party governments. This, rather than economics, he saw as the root of the instability from 1948 onwards. He considered that the straight vote would produce decisive election results and would be conducive to a return to strong government.[7]

Whatever the weaknesses or simplicities of Fianna Fáil economic policy from 1932, it could at least claim to be the original Sinn Féin policy. To have abandoned that policy without testing it would probably have been more culpable than testing it and failing. What de Valera could be accused of, however, is persisting with the old orthodoxies long after they had been found wanting. One of the remarkable features of the economic crisis which engulfed the Irish state in the fifteen years after the Second World War is how slow the state was to respond. Dr T. K. Whitaker's *Economic Development,* published in 1958, said little which had not been widely rehearsed over the previous decade; it is hard to avoid the conclusion that, like an extinct volcano, de Valera's lingering on in power after the reverses of 1948 and 1954 hindered the pace of change. Remarkably, the section of de Valera's official biography dealing with the post-war years is entitled 'The Stable Years'—this of a period during which half a million emigrated in fifteen years. Had de Valera retired in 1945, at the height of his power, the verdict of history might be kinder and the lives of a lost generation of Irish emigrants might have been very different.

The new economic policy embarked upon from 1957 ensured that the retirement of de Valera and the succession of Lemass marked more than simply a change in personnel. Lemass's nationalist credentials were unimpeachable, but his urban orienation and his appetite for economic expansion ensured that the tone of his party and government would be markedly different from de Valera's. The restless, rapidly changing Ireland of the 1960s and 1970s was in stark contrast to that of the preceding decades. To see Lemass as the main instigator of this change would be simplistic: to speak of Lemass's Ireland is as misleading as speaking of de Valera's Ireland; but there is no doubt that the change of economic direction followed so soon by the retirement of de Valera marked the end of one era and the beginning of another.

While he retired from active politics, de Valera did not retire from public life. In June 1959 he was elected President of Ireland and held that position with some distinction for two seven-year terms until his retirement in 1973. He made a number of foreign visits, including a visit to the United States for the funeral of John F. Kennedy in 1963, a visit to Rome for the coronation of Pope Paul VI, and a state visit to the United States and Canada in 1964, when he addressed a joint session of Congress.

In his 1937 constitution, no doubt mindful of the German experience, de Valera had been careful to make the role of the President largely ceremonial. In this it differered radically from the American and French presidencies. It was never likely, therefore, that he would himself seek to exercise a direct political influence. In 1969 he helped to avert a crisis within the government when he persuaded Kevin Boland to withdraw a threat to resign in protest against the Lynch government's northern policy. In the event, Boland later resigned and Lynch dismissed two other senior ministers, Neil Blaney and Charles J. Haughey, over their alleged involvement in gun-running to Northern Ireland. At a time when the course of events in Northern Ireland posed a considerable challenge to the government, Lynch hoped that the President would issue a condemnation of the I.R.A.'s military campaign, but de Valera declined to become involved publicly.[8] Towards the end of his second term of office he became increasingly inactive. In 1973, having served the maximum allowable two terms, he retired as President. He died on 29 August 1975.

# CONCLUSION

If, as suggested at the outset, he will be judged by future historians mainly on what he did after rather than before 1922, how stands de Valera? There is no doubt that he did come to embody Irish independence for many. As the senior survivor of the 1916 rising, he represented the strongest link with the spirit of that rebellion and those who sacrificed themselves then or in the War of Independence. Despite the vicissitudes of later years, especially the Treaty split, and the elusiveness of the promised land once in power, that link strengthened rather than weakened with the passage of time. His followers remained intensely loyal.

At the same time, de Valera remained for some a divisive figure. The Treaty split and Civil War became and remained at least until the 1960s the main arbiter of political loyalties in Ireland and determined the political allegiances of two generations. These allegiances were virtually solidified as Irish politics fossilised into pro- and anti-Treaty camps. Not surprisingly, those who supported the Treaty and their successors in Cumann na nGaedheal and, later, Fine Gael, did not share the view of de Valera as the embodiment of independence. Nor did the passage of time dim their hostility: the fact that in 1966 Fine Gael considered it necessary to put forward a candidate against the eighty-four-year-old elder statesman when he sought re-election as President, and that, out of the one million votes cast, de Valera's majority was only 20,000 emphasises the extent to which he remained until the end a divisive figure.

The critics of de Valera were not confined to Cumann na nGaedheal and Fine Gael. The Treaty split temporarily masked the differences between the dogmatic republicans and the more pragmatic de Valera. These differences quickly re-emerged and manifested themselves during the Civil War and later culminated in his break with Sinn Féin. Sinn Féin and the I.R.A. continue to dispute any claim that de Valera inherited the mantle of 1916. His strong action against the I.R.A. during the Second World War and in the 1950s, when leading republicans were interned, only served to harden their position.

48

A third, rather more heterogeneous group who challenged the hegemony of de Valera were social critics, intellectuals and radicals who rejected the narrowness of de Valera's vision and deplored the backwardness of the country he ruled. Some of these were initially sympathetic but became disillusioned when he failed to turn ideals into reality or when the reality seemed too unpalatable. The success of Clann na Poblachta in 1948 was fuelled mainly by this current.

It is hard to quibble with Ronan Fanning's assessment that de Valera's ultimate achievements were political sovereignty and psychological independence.[1] To that list might be added the Fianna Fáil party and its contribution to the entrenching of stable democratic politics in Ireland from the 1920s. De Valera contributed to a sense of self-reliance and national identity and, despite the Civil War, to the establishment of political stability. In the light of the experience of other comparable countries, that achievement is not to be underestimated. Whatever the dismalness of the de Valera vision, political democracy emerged unscathed and even strengthened from his hegemony, which is more than can be said for many post-colonial societies and indeed much of Europe during the same period.

De Valera failed to end partition, but it would be unreasonable to expect that a single politician, however powerful, might have done otherwise. Early in his career he briefly entertained the possibility of coercion, but thereafter his policy was more pragmatic and reasonable than he is often given credit for. De Valera's anti-partition campaign after 1948 might be accused of being opportunist, but probably the major criticism that might be levelled against him is that the state he helped to create proved so unattractive in social and economic terms to northern Protestants.

De Valera once advised Richard Mulcahy that if he intended to enter politics, he should study Machiavelli and read economics.[2] It is no criticism to say that he himself mastered Machiavelli better than Keynes. He was an accomplished political tactician, but underestimated the importance of economics. He failed to create economic prosperity or end emigration, but in weighing that failure one must consider the strength of the underlying forces over which he had no control. The protectionist policies adopted from 1932 provided the environment in which native Irish industries might be nourished. In the light of the relative underdevelopment of Ireland at the time and the restrictive policies being adopted elsewhere in the 1930s, protection was probably the most viable policy for Ireland. By the 1950s the international context had changed, but Fianna Fáil was slow to adapt, with considerable implications for a generation of Irish emigrants. When the change of direction did come, it proved spectacularly successful and, *inter alia*, served to maintain Fianna Fáil in power for another sixteen years.

In international affairs de Valera rapidly transcended the British portrayal of him as a dangerous fanatic and established himself as a significant international statesman. He was the only Irish leader of his generation to have such a profile. Abroad, even more than at home, he was the personification of the Irish struggle for independence. He became a hero for independence movements elsewhere, for example in India. His espousal of the cause of small countries through the League of Nations, his maintenance of Irish neutrality against strong outside pressure and his championing of the non-aligned movement pointed the way forward for newly emerging countries.

When asked by an interviewer late in his life what his greatest regret was, de Valera cited not the Treaty split or partition, but his failure to revive Irish. He certainly had a deeper commitment to the Irish language than any other leader since 1922, believing, like Thomas Davis, that 'a people without a language of its own is only half a nation'.[3] He was personally responsible for putting the weight of the state behind the revival movement. Whether that helped or hindered the movement might be debated. Certainly de Valera accepted that despite the official imprimatur, the revival had made disappointing progress by the end of his life. He concluded that without widespread popular support, the movement could not succeed. Government support and endorsement were 'auxiliary aids':

> The restoration of the language can only be brought about by the active desire of a sufficiently large number of people to learn the language and their untiring, persevering assiduity in using what they learn. You can bring a horse to the water, or

the water to the horse, but you cannot make him drink. The one thing that is needed at the moment is the stimulus to activate the desire to drink.[4]

His somewhat remote, schoolmasterish manner contributed to de Valera's undoubted charisma and was probably well suited to his role in foreign affairs, but it could pose problems for those who had to deal with him at close quarters, not least his own colleagues. In government he devolved too little and interfered too much, but even his opponents admitted he was an extraordinary man. In 1934, writing to J. H. Thomas, the British Secretary of State for the Dominions who liked to call de Valera the 'Spanish onion in the Irish stew', Lord Granard tried to sum up a politician he found exasperating, infuriating, but deeply impressive:

> I have known Mr de Valera only very slightly up to now. He is a most curious personality, very pleasant socially and possessed of good manners. But he is certainly not normal. He is on the borderline between genius and insanity. I have met men of many countries and have been Governor of a Lunatic Asylum, but I have never met anybody like the President of the Executive Council of the Irish Free State before. I hope that the Almighty does not create any more of the same pattern and that he will remain content with this one example.[5]

# NOTES

## Introduction

[1] I am indebted to Eoghan Ó Súilleabháin for the details of this story. It was told to him by his uncle, Seán Ó Súilleabháin.

[2] For a list of the major works on de Valera see the Select Bibliography below.

## 1

[1] The unusual circumstances of de Valera's birth and parentage have given rise over the years to considerable speculation and rumour, fuelled no doubt also by his political opponents. Despite his intensive rooting into this area, Coogan has added little to what is known or verifiable. Tim Pat Coogan, *De Valera: Long Fellow, Long Shadow* (London, 1993), pp 3–9. For the official version of these years see Earl of Longford and T. P. O'Neill, *Eamon de Valera* (London, 1970), pp 1–3.

[2] On the outlook of Irish nationalists see Tom Garvin, *The Evolution of Irish Nationalist Politics* (Dublin, 1981).

[3] Desmond Ryan, *Unique Dictator: A Study of Eamon de Valera* (London, 1936), p. 7.

[4] *Dáil Treaty Deb.*, 6 Jan. 1922, p. 274.

[5] Sean O'Faolain, *The Life Story of Eamon de Valera* (Dublin, 1933), p. 108; Erhard Rumpf and A. C. Hepburn, *Nationalism and Socialism in Twentieth-Century Ireland* (Liverpool, 1977), p. 98.

[6] Longford and O'Neill, *De Valera*, p. 9.

[7] *Dáil Treaty Deb.*, 6 Jan. 1922, p. 281.

[8] Inaugural address at La Scala Theatre, 16 May 1926, repr. in Maurice Moynihan (ed.), *Speeches and Statements of Eamon de Valera, 1917-73* (Dublin, 1980), pp 133–42.

[9] O'Faolain, *De Valera*, pp 9, 102; Rumpf and Hepburn, *Nationalism and Socialism*, p. 98.

[10] William O'Brien, *The Irish Revolution* (Dublin, 1928), pp 361–2.

[11] Quoted in Longford and O'Neill, *De Valera*, p. xxi.

## 2

[1] Longford and O'Neill, *De Valera*, p. 25.

[2] Ibid., pp 25–6, 33–4.

[3] Ibid., pp 37–50.

[4] For a full, if not fully persuasive, discussion of these allegations see Coogan, *De Valera*, pp 68–74. The case rests mainly on the evidence of Simon Donnelly, for which see his memoir, 'Mount St Bridge' (Franciscan Archives, Killiney, de Valera papers, Folders 29C, E).

[5] Coogan, *De Valera*, p. 78.

[6] Longford and O'Neill, *De Valera*, p. 64.

[7] Dorothy Macardle, *The Irish Republic* (London, 1937), p. 217.

[8] PRO, CO 904/23/3, pp 44, 104.

[9] On the conscription crisis see Pauric Travers, 'The Irish Conscription Crisis' (unpublished M.A. thesis, University College, Dublin, 1978).

[10] NLI, Minutes of Sinn Féin Standing Committee, 18–9 Apr. 1918; PRO, CO 903/19, p. 5; Collins Diary, Apr. 1918. See 'The Prison Diary of Michael Collins', *Studia Hibernica*, xxviii (1994).

[11] Longford and O'Neill, *De Valera*, pp 95–114; T. Ryle Dwyer, *Eamon de Valera* (Dublin, 1980), pp 21–38.

[12] Dwyer, *De Valera*, p. 41.

[13] Dáil cabinet meetings, 15 Sept., 25 Nov. 1921, (NA, DE 1/3); Michael Hopkinson, *Green Against Green: The Irish Civil War* (Dublin, 1988), pp 14–18.

[14] Thomas Jones, *Whitehall Diary*, iii: *Ireland, 1918–25*, ed. Keith Middlemass (London, 1971), p. 60; Mark Sturgis Diary, 13 June 1921 (PRO, 39/50/4).

[15] Longford and O'Neill, *De Valera*, p. 138; Dwyer, *De Valera*, p. 43.

[16] De Valera to Lloyd George, 19 Sept. 1921 (House of Lords Record Office, Lloyd George Papers, F/14/6.

[17] Lloyd George to de Valera, 29 Sept. 1921; de Valera to Lloyd George, 30 Sept. 1921 (Lloyd George Papers, F/14/6).

[18] Oliver MacDonagh, *Ireland, the Union and its Aftermath* (London, 1977), p. 106.

[19] Ronan Fanning, *Independent Ireland* (Dublin, 1983), p. 3.

[20] Dwyer, *De Valera*, p. 53.

[21] O'Connell Diary, 7 Dec. 1921 (de Valera Papers, Killiney, Folder 1473/1).

[22] Dwyer, *De Valera*, p. 55. See 'Irish proposals, Treaty, 1921' (de Valera Papers, Killiney, Folder 168).

[23] *Dáil Treaty Deb.*, 7 Dec. 1921, p. 347; Jennie Wyse Power to Nancy Wyse Power, 8 Jan 1922, quoted in Marie O'Neill, *From Parnell to de Valera: A Biography of Jennie Wyse Power, 1858–1941* (Dublin, 1991), p. 132.

[24] *Dáil Private Sess.*, pp 121, 137.

[25] Ibid., pp 27–9.

[26] Moynihan (ed.), *Speeches and Statements*, pp 97–102.

[27] The best account of the drift into civil war is Michael Hopkinson, *Green Against Green* (Dublin, 1988).

### 3

[1] Longford and O'Neill, *De Valera*, p. 217; Dwyer, *De Valera*, p. 70.

[2] For an analysis of the Sinn Féin vote in 1923 see Rumpf and Hepburn, *Nationalism and Socialism*, p. 60.

[3] Maurice Manning, *Irish Political Parties*, Studies in Irish Political Culture, 3 (Dublin, 1972), p. 36.

[4] Peter Pyne, 'The Third Sinn Fein Party', *Economic and Social Review*, i, no. 1, (Oct. 1969), pp 36–46.

[5] Rumpf and Hepburn, *Nationalism and Socialism*, p. 100.

[6] Longford and O'Neill, *De Valera*, pp 254–5.

[7] *Dáil Deb.*, xxii, 1615–16.

[8] Rumpf and Hepburn, *Nationalism and Socialism*, pp 104–8.

### 4

[1] On the British attitude to de Valera and Fianna Fáil see Deirdre McMahon, 'A Transient Apparition: British Policy towards the de Valera Government, 1932–5', *Irish Historical Studies*, xxii, no. 88 (Sept. 1981), pp 332–61.

[2] Cormac Ó Gráda, *Ireland: A New Economic History, 1780–1939* (Oxford, 1994), p. 416.

[3] Mary E. Daly, *Social and Economic History of Ireland since 1800* (Dublin, 1981), pp 148–51.

[4] Ibid., pp 155, 152.

[5] Ó Gráda, *Ireland*, p. 398.

[6] Moynihan (ed.), *Speeches and Statements*, p. 222.

[7] *Peace and War: Speeches by Mr de Valera on International Affairs* (Dublin, 1944), pp 45–8.

[8] *Dáil Deb.*, lxii, 2654–60; Moynihan (ed.), *Speeches and Statements*, pp 273–7.

[9] Moynihan (ed.), *Speeches and Statements*, pp 282–5.

[10] *Dáil Deb.*, lxiv, 1217–24; Moynihan (ed.), *Speeches and Statements*, pp 285–9.

[11] Moynihan (ed.), *Speeches and Statements*, pp 470–75.

[12] Radio broadcast, 17 Mar. 1941 (Moynihan (ed.), *Speeches and Statements*, p. 452).

[13] John A. Murphy, *Ireland in the Twentieth Century* (Dublin, 1975), pp 99–107; Fanning, *Independent Ireland*, p. 120; F. S. L. Lyons, *Ireland since the Famine* (London, 1971), p. 551.

[14] See, for example, Cranborne memorandum, 21 Feb. 1945 (PRO, CAB 66/62; cited in Fanning, *Independent Ireland*, p. 124).

[15] Murphy, *Ireland in the Twentieth Century*, p. 107.

[16] J. J. Lee, *Ireland, 1912–1985* (Cambridge, 1989), pp 258–70.

5

[1] See, for example, Fanning, *Independent Ireland*, ch. 3; R. F. Foster, *Modern Ireland, 1600–1972* (London,1988), ch. 22.

[2] *The Bell*, xx, no. 1 (Apr. 1945), pp 11–12.

[3] *Irish Press*, 2 Jan., 2, 3 Feb., 17 Mar. 1948; Moynihan (ed.), *Speeches and Statements*, p. 556. For de Valera and emigration see 'The Dream Gone Bust: Irish Responses to Emigration 1922-60' in Oliver MacDonagh and W. F. Mandle (eds), *Irish-Australian Studies* (Canberra, 1989), pp 318–42.

[4] 'Early Marriage: Encouragement among Farmers' (National Archives of Ireland, S13413/1). On the dower house scheme and social conditions in this period see Pauric Travers, 'Irish Female Emigration, 1922–71' forthcoming in the Proceedings of the 1993 Irish Conference of Historians, ed. Mary O'Dowd (Institute of Irish Studies, Belfast, spring 1995).

[5] F. W. Stock, 17 Jan. 1944 (cited in Travers, 'Irish Female Emigration').

[6] Longford and O'Neill, *De Valera*, p. 470.

[7] John Bowman, *De Valera and the Ulster Question* (Oxford, 1982), p. 305.

[8] *Freeman's Journal*, 30 Jan. 1918.

[9] St John Ervine, *Craigavon: Ulsterman* (London, 1949), p. 411. Kathleen O'Connell noted in her diary that Craig was frightened and de Valera amused, 5 May 1921 (de Valera Papers, Folder 1473/1).

[10] De Valera to Lloyd George, 19 July 1921 (House of Lords Record Office, Lloyd George Papers, F/14/6/11); De Valera to Lloyd George, 10 Aug. 1921 (*Dáil Éireann: Official Correspondence relating to Peace Negotiations*, p. 11).

[11] *Dáil Private Sess.*, pp 28–35.

[12] Frank Pakenham, *Peace by Ordeal* (London, 1935), p. 209; *Dáil Private Sess.*, pp 317–24; Bowman, *De Valera and the Ulster Question*, pp 63–9; 'Document Number 2' (de Valera Papers, Folders, 1937–9).

[13] *Irish Independent*, 18 Nov. 1925.

[14] *Irish Times*, 26 Nov. 1926.

[15] *Sunday Press*, 4 Apr. 1953.

[16] Bowman, *De Valera and the Ulster Question*, p. 312.

[17] *Dáil Deb.*, xlvi, 192, (1 Mar. 1932); quoted in Clare O'Halloran, *Partition and the Limits of Irish Nationalism* (Dublin, 1987), pp 162–3.

[18] See, for example, Dermot Keogh, *Twentieth-Century Ireland: Nation and State* (Dublin, 1994), p. 69.

[19] For a good recent discussion see ibid., pp 68–70.

[20] *Round Table*, xxv (1934–5), p. 551 .

[21] *Irish Independent*, 14 Mar. 1925; quoted in Lee, *Ireland*, p. 161.

[22] McQuaid to de Valera, 23 Feb. 1944 (cited in T. P. O'Neill, 'Dr J. C. McQuaid and Eamon de Valera: Insights on Church and State', *Breifne*, viii, no.3, (1992–3), p. 329.

[23] Ibid.

[24] Ibid.

[25] Ibid., p. 344; Eamon McKee, 'Church–State Relations and the Development of Irish Health Policy: the Mother and Child Scheme, 1944–53', *Irish Historical Studies*, xxv, no. 98 (Nov. 1986), pp 159–94.

[26] Gertrude Gaffney, 'A Woman's View of the Constitution', *Irish Independent*, 7 May 1937.

[27] O'Faolain, *De Valera*, pp 110–11.

[28] Quoted in Dwyer, *De Valera*, p. 96.

[29] Gaffney, 'A Woman's View of the Constitution'.

[30] Moynihan (ed.), *Speeches and Statements*, pp 466–9. The words used in the broadcast were slightly different than the later text used by Moynihan, but not in any substantive way.

# 6

[1] MacDonagh, *Ireland*, p. 119.

[2] *The Bell*, xiv, no. 5 (Aug. 1947), pp 1–3.

[3] Speech in New York, 3 Apr. 1948 (Moynihan (ed.), *Speeches and Statements* pp 497–504).

[4] Dáil Éireann, 24 Nov., 1 Dec. 1948 (quoted ibid., pp 505–20).

[5] Paul Bew and Henry Patterson, *Seán Lemass and the Making of Modern Ireland, 1945–66* (Dublin, 1982), pp 64–6.

[6] Interview with Michael Mills, *Irish Press*, 27 Jan. 1969.

[7] Speech in Dáil Éireann, 26 Nov. 1958 (quoted in Moynihan (ed.), *Speeches and Statements*, pp 589–94).

[8] Dwyer, *De Valera* p. 146.

## Conclusion

[1] Fanning, *Independent Ireland*, pp 190–91.

[2] Longford and O'Neill, *De Valera*, p. 88.

[3] For de Valera and the Irish language see Dáithí Ó hÓgáin, 'De Valera agus Cultúr na nDaoine', *Inniu*, 22 Oct. 1972. See also his speech at Mansion House, 7 Feb. 1949, a typed copy of which he carefully preserved in his papers; most of the text is reproduced in Moynihan (ed.), *Speeches and Statements*, pp 522–7.

[4] Moynihan (ed.) , *Speeches and Statements*, pp 523–4.

[5] Robert Fisk, *In Time of War* (London, 1983), p. 26; Irish Situation Committee, 28 Aug. 1934 (PRO, CAB 27/526).

# SELECT BIBLIOGRAPHY

Bowman, John, *De Valera and the Ulster Question, 1917–1973* (Oxford, 1982)

Bromage, Mary C., *De Valera and the March of a Nation* (London, 1956)

Coogan, Tim Pat, *De Valera: Long Fellow, Long Shadow* (London, 1993)

Dwyer, T. Ryle, *Eamon de Valera* (Dublin, 1980)

Dwyer, T. Ryle, *De Valera: the Man and the Myths* (Dublin, 1991)

Edwards, Owen Dudley, *Eamon de Valera* (Cardiff, 1987).

Farrell, Brian, (ed.), *De Valera's Constitution and Ours* (Dublin, 1988)

Fitzgibbon, Constantine, *The Life and Times of Eamon de Valera* (Dublin, 1973).

Gwynn, Denis, *De Valera* (London, 1933)

Hopkinson, Michael, *Green Against Green: The Irish Civil War* (Dublin, 1988)

Keogh, Dermot, *Twentieth-Century Ireland: Nation and State* (Dublin, 1994)

Lee, J. J., *Ireland, 1912–1985* (Cambridge, 1989)

Lee, J. J., and Ó Tuathaigh, Gearóid, *The Age of de Valera* (Dublin, 1982)

Longford, Earl of, and O'Neill, T.P., *Eamon de Valera* (1970)

Lyons, F. S. L., 'Symbol of the Era He Bestrode' in *Irish Times, Eamon de Valera, 1882–1975* (Dublin, 1976)

Macardle, Dorothy, *The Irish Republic* (London, 1937)

McCartan, Patrick, *With de Valera in America* (New York, 1932)

McMahon, Deirdre, *Republicans and Imperialists: Anglo-Irish Relations in the 1930s* (London, 1984)

McManus, M. J., *Eamon de Valera* (Dublin, 1957)

Moynihan, Maurice, (ed.), *Speeches and Statements by Eamon de Valera, 1917–73* (Dublin, 1980)

O'Carroll, J. P., and Murphy, J. A., *De Valera and His Times* (Cork, 1983)

O'Faolain, Seán, *The Life Story of Eamon de Valera* (Dublin, 1933)

Ó Gráda, Cormac, *Ireland: A New Economic History 1780–1939* (Oxford, 1994)

O'Neill, T. P., and Ó Fiannachta Pádraig, *De Valera* (2 vols. Dublin, 1968–70)

Pakenham, Frank, *Peace by Ordeal* (London, 1935)

Ryan, Desmond, *Unique Dictator: A Study of Eamon de Valera* (London, 1936)

Williams, T. D., *The Irish Struggle, 1916–26* (London, 1966)